# MUHAMMAD
## The Last Prophet

Uzma Ausaf

An imprint of Om Books International

First Published in 2020 by

## Om KIDZ | Om Books International

**Corporate & Editorial Office**
A-12, Sector 64, Noida 201 301
Uttar Pradesh, India
Phone: +91 120 477 4100
Email: editorial@ombooks.com
Website: www.ombooksinternational.com

© Om Books International 2020
Author: Uzma Ausaf
Editor: Apoorva Kaul
Art & Design: Manoj Prasad, Gaurav Bhandari, Arijit Ganguly

ISBN: 978-93-5376-001-4

Printed in India
10 9 8 7 6 5 4 3 2 1

**Sales Office**
107, Ansari Road, Darya Ganj
New Delhi 110 002, India
Phone: +91 11 4000 9000
Email: sales@ombooks.com
Website: www.ombooks.com

# Contents

# Early Days

Muhammad was the last Prophet of Islam. He was born in Makkah in AD 570. His father Abdullah ibn Abdul Muttalib died before Muhammad was born. The young boy lost his mother Aminah by the time he turned six, and his grandfather Abdul Muttalib soon after. Muhammad was then brought up and cared for by his uncle Talib.

The two shared a strong bond, which lasted even after Muhammad had become a prophet at the age of 40.

Muhammad was a thoughtful child. Wise beyond his years, he spent long hours in solitude, pondering over the reason for existence while grazing goats. Known for his integrity, he never picked fights with anyone and sought peaceful solutions to every problem. Muhammad was also called Ahmad, which meant "the Praised One".

As a young man, the unlettered Muhammad travelled with his uncle in trade caravans and gained fame for being fair while conducting business successfully.

# Noticed by Khadijah

Khadijah was a business woman whose wealth exceeded that of the combined wealth of the richest men of her time. When she heard stories of Muhammad's business acumen and sense of fair play, she hired him to lead a trade caravan to Syria, where he made good profit for her.

Once, while conducting business, a man named Maysara accompanied Muhammad. When Muhammad sat down under a tree to rest, Nustoor, a Christian priest, approached Maysara and enquired about Muhammad. Nustoor predicted that Muhammad would become the last Prophet of Allah.

Unaware of any such prediction, the twice widowed Khadijah married Muhammad, 15 years her junior. This made the other rich men who had wanted to marry Khadijah resent Muhammad. Theirs was a happy marriage. They were blessed with four daughters.

# The Prophet Goes to the Cave

Muhammad was of a spiritual disposition. For moments of peace and quiet, he would retire to the Cave of Hira. Khadijah brought food for him when he meditated in the cave. On one such night, the angel Jibrail visited Muhammad. Muhammad started trembling. Jibrail asked Muhammad to read but Muhammad could not. Jibrail then made Muhammad repeat after him, *"Iqra Bismikallazi..."* This is the first verse of the Quran. The angel left and Muhammad came down from the cave, shivering.

Khadijah believed Muhammad, becoming the first woman to embrace Islam. It was AD 610 and 40-year-old Muhammad had become a prophet, the last in a line that had begun with Adam. Isa, another prophet, had foreseen this 600 years ago.

# Beginning of a Revolution

Jibrail taught Muhammad how to perform ablutions before prayer and how to pray. Muhammad then taught these to his wife, his cousin Ali, his adopted son Zaid and Abu Bakr, one of his most faithful companions. Muslims continue to follow these practices across the world, even today.

Unlike other prophets, Muhammad was a guiding light for the entire humanity. Muhammad preached the worship of one Allah who has no equal, no father and no child. In the beginning, Muhammad and his companions prayed outside Makkah. They did not announce their religion to everyone, but looked for people they believed to be reasonable and honest.

Gradually, people came to know that Muhammad was claiming to be a prophet and that he preached the worship of only one God. This challenged the religious views of the

non-believers of the Arab world who worshipped their family deities like Lat, Naila and Uzza. For three years, the Prophet preached quietly to a few individuals after which he began inviting common people to the fold of Islam.

Once, he laid out a feast and invited all his near and dear ones. He planned to introduce them to Islam at the end of the meal. However, his uncle, Abu Lahab rallied everyone against Muhammad by telling them that Muhammad had abandoned the religion of his forefathers

and started a new faith. In the din, Muhammad's voice could not be heard. Sometime later, he organised another feast. With their minds already set against Muhammad's teachings, everyone left the feast, leaving behind just a teenage boy.

Muhammad then climbed a hill as is customary in the Arab world, and warned the people of danger. "O people of Quraish, protect yourself from the anger of Allah. There is only a single

way to protect from hellfire. And it is that you accept Allah as the Only One to worship, and accept me as His messenger." Islam was beginning to grow as a religion.

# Companions Go to Ethiopia

The non-believers continued to harass the Prophet. They would throw stones at him; many would toss night soil in front of his house. Two of his daughters who were married to sons of Abu Lahab suffered as Abu Lahab asked his sons to leave them. However, this did not deter the Prophet.

As Muhammad's fame grew, so did his enemies. One day, when Muhammad was praying, his enemy Abu Jahl tried to smash Muhammad's head with a stone. Every time Abu Jahl lifted the stone, a terrible fire would emerge in front of him, compelling him to drop the stone. However, Muhammad's companions faced social and economic boycott.

Followers like Yasir, Sumayya and Ammar were tortured by the enemies of Islam, with Sumayya becoming the first martyr of Islam. The Prophet told them to go to Ethiopia, ruled by King Negus who was known for his fair judgment. Eleven men and four women went

by boat, but the Quraish chased them and asked King Negus to deport them. The king gave audience to the migrants and asked them to tell him about the Quran.

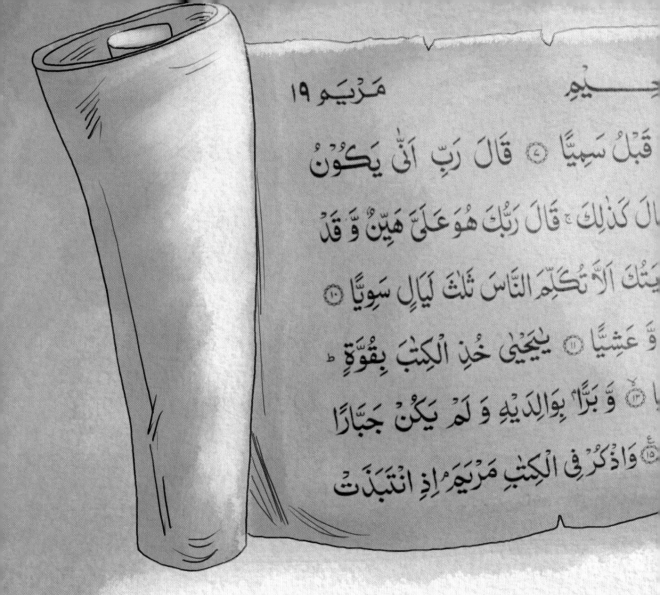

مَرْيَمَ ۱۹ ... حِيمٌ

قَبْلُ سَمِيًّا ۞ قَالَ رَبِّ اَنّٰى يَكُوْنُ

...الَ كَذٰلِكَ ۚ قَالَ رَبُّكَ هُوَ عَلَيَّ هَيِّنٌ ۚ وَّ قَدْ

...يْتُكَ اَلَّا تُكَلِّمَ النَّاسَ ثَلٰثَ لَيَالٍ سَوِيًّا ۞

وَّ عَشِيًّا ۞ يٰيَحْيٰى خُذِ الْكِتٰبَ بِقُوَّةٍ ط

...بِا ۞ وَّ بَرًّا بِوَالِدَيْهِ وَ لَمْ يَكُنْ جَبَّارًا

...ۤا ۞ وَاذْكُرْ فِى الْكِتٰبِ مَرْيَمَ ۚ اِذِ انْتَبَذَتْ

The Quran had begun to be revealed in AD 610, and the revelations had been memorised by many by now. On hearing the *Surah Maryam*, which talked of the supremacy of Allah, and His help towards

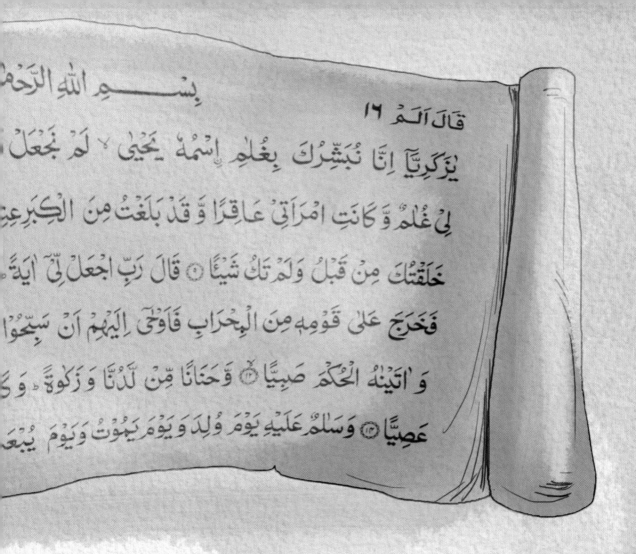

all prophets and common believers alike, the king had tears streaming down his cheeks. He gave the Muslim migrants full protection and it is through them that Islam spread to the rest of Africa.

# Year of Sorrow

One night, three members of the Quraish clan, Abu Jahl, Abu Sufyan and Akhnas came to the Prophet's house and sat by the wall, unaware of each other's presence. They listened to his recitation of the Quran. As dawn approached, they saw each other. They knew Muhammad's message was true but still did not accept him, as that would have led to loss of their social standing. They continued to defy the Prophet and bar Muslims from trade.

With more and more Muslims migrating to Ethiopia, Muhammad had only a few followers left with him in Makkah. In Makkah, the Muslims faced starvation but were helped by Muhammad's uncle Talib,

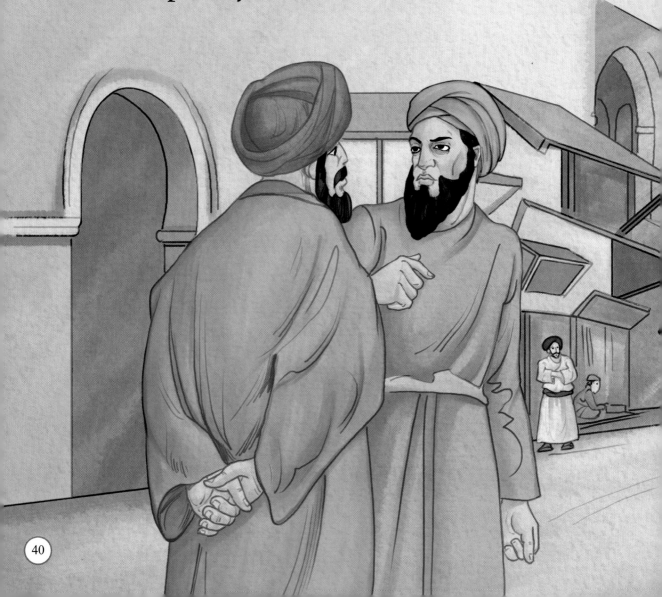

his wife Khadijah, his new companion Umar and his son Hisham who brought food and clothing for the Muslims in the dead of night. With their help, Muslims came out of confinement and their economic boycott began to end.

The 10th year of Muhammad's enlightenment was one of immense personal grief for him. His uncle Talib fell ill and passed away. Soon after, his wife Khadijah, who had supported him all along also died. These losses did not deter Muhammad.

43

# Turned Away from Taif

Leaving his sorrows behind him, the Prophet married Saudah, and later Aisha. The torture inflicted on him by the non-believers forced him to migrate to Taif, some 60 miles from Makkah. However, the people of Taif worshipped Lat and did not allow Muhammad to stay there. Rogue elements threw stones at him. Bleeding, Muhammad reached the orchard of Utba and Shebah, the sons of Rabiah, a believer.

The brothers saw his suffering and asked their slave Addas to give him some grapes for comfort. Muhammad accepted the offering with an invocation to Allah, "I begin in the name of Allah, the Most Merciful."

These words moved Addas, a Christian. "You are a follower of Yunus, who was a prophet," said Muhammad. "I am a prophet, too." Addas kissed Muhammad's forehead and related the story to his masters.

On his way back to Makkah, Muhammad halted for a night at Nakhlah. The *jinns* heard him reciting the Quran and embraced Islam. However, the non-believers pursued Muhammad, wanting to eliminate him. A kind man named Mutim granted him shelter, and the Prophet started going to nearby villages to preach the word of Allah.

# Journey Across Mairaj

Prophet Muhammad decided to spend some time at the house of his cousin Hind, Abu Talib's daughter. He offered *Isha* prayers with Hind one night, and the next morning he offered *Fajr* prayers with her too. In between, he went on *Mairaj*, a journey across seven heavens. Hind then asked him how he had managed to do this. "When I was sleeping, Jibrail came through the roof, and took me to Hatim at Kaaba," said Muhammad.

Hatim is a place where no prayer goes unanswered. "He tore my chest. He had a gold saucer. He poured its contents on my chest and sealed it. Then a white animal, a little smaller than a horse, came. We rode on it. Within minutes, we reached Baitul Muqaddas – the purest House of Allah. There

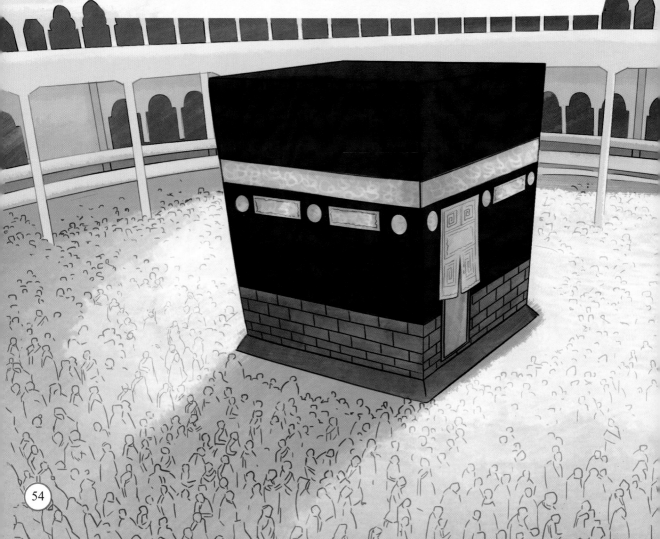

I offered prayers, and all the prophets prayed behind me." Thus took place Prophet Muhammad's famed journey across the seven heavens during which he saw all the prophets who came before him and also the scenes of heaven and hell. He led the other prophets in prayers too.

Hind advised him not to tell the Quraish clan of his journey, as they would not believe him. Muhammad refused, saying, "Allah's help is enough for us." At Kaaba, he told everyone about his journey, but only Abu Bakr and a few others believed him.

Ridiculed by many, the Prophet continued preaching the word of Allah, attracting people from Makkah and beyond. The Khizraj tribe from Madinah embraced Islam, adding that the local Jews had told them about his arrival. They went back home and

the faith grew as others in Madinah accepted it as well. Within a year, the number of Muslims in Madinah had exceeded that of Makkah. The people of Madinah invited the Prophet to their land and he accepted.

# I439 ISLAMIC CALENDAR

**2018**
*9 جنوری*

**34**

| | SUN | 1 | 8 | 15 | 22 | 29 |
| | MON | 2 | 9 | 16 | 23 | 30 |
| | TUE | 3 | 10 | 17 | 24 | |
| | WED | 4 | 11 | 18 | 25 | |
| | THU | 5 | 12 | 19 | 26 | |
| | FRI | 6 | 13 | 20 | 27 | |
| | SAT | 7 | 14 | 21 | 28 | |

# Hijrat to Madinah

Soon, a divine order came from Allah for *Hijrat* – migration. In small groups of twos and threes, Muslims started migrating from Makkah to Madinah. This marked the beginning of the Hijri Islamic calendar.

All the Muslims quietly migrated. Muhammad waited with Abu Bakr for Allah's orders. The Quraish tribe of Makkah felt threatened. They felt the Prophet would attack them with the support of the Madinah tribes. They plotted to kill Muhammad. Then Allah ordered the Prophet to leave for Madinah. The Quraish

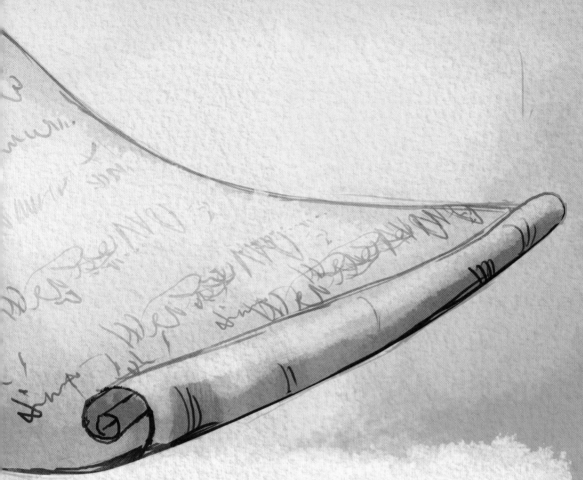

surrounded his house. As Muhammad was the custodian of the wealth for some local people, he asked his cousin Ali to return it to them and then join the Prophet. As he stepped out, the Prophet quoted the *Surah Yasin*, which is recited at a moment of great difficulty, and threw a handful of dust at the Quraish, blinding them for a while.

The Prophet reached Abu Bakr's house where his wife, Aishaa, who happened to be Abu Bakr's daughter, waited for him. Muhammad and Abu Bakr went in the opposite direction of Madinah to avoid their enemies. However, the Quraish captured Ali and beat him mercilessly, before a relative saved him.

Suraqa who could read footprints, led the Quraish, who were searching for the Prophet, to a cave. The attackers reached the cave where Prophet Muhammad was praying to Allah and saw what appeared to be an old spider's web. They retreated, believing no spider would build a web at a place frequented by human beings.

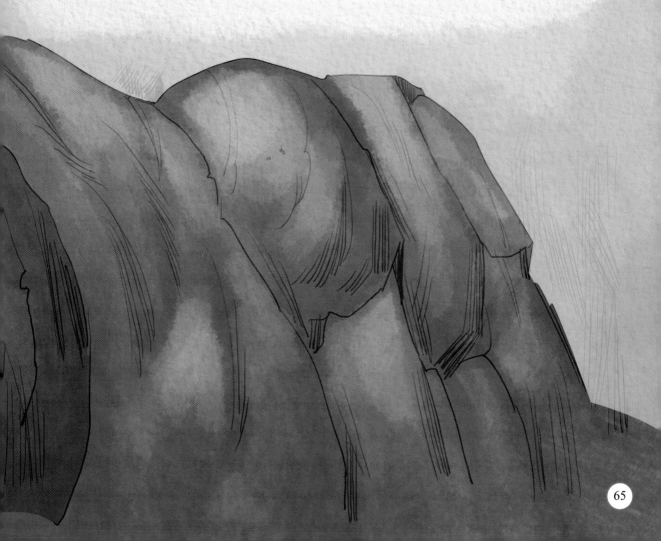

The Prophet and Abu Bakr left the cave on camelback, travelling an entire day without a break, after which the Prophet rested under some shade. Unknown to them, a rider had been following. On seeing the Prophet resting, the rider galloped towards them. However, his

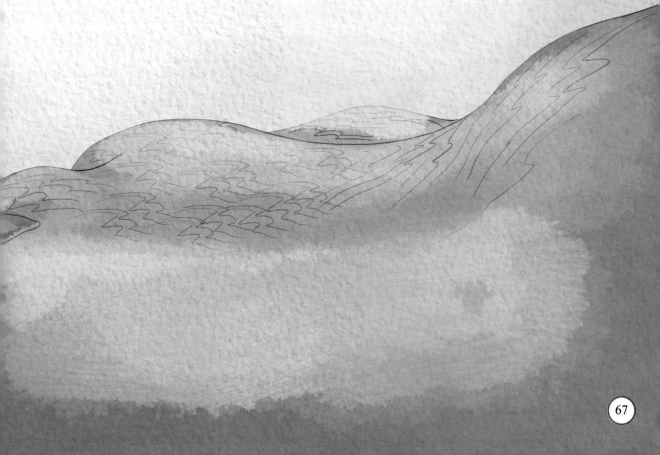

horse's legs gave way in the sand, throwing him forward. Realising that he was not destined to capture the Prophet, he sought the Prophet's forgiveness.

The Prophet and his companion reunited with Ali in Quba, a small village near Madinah. At Quba, the Prophet laid the foundation of the first mosque.

The Prophet reached Madinah on a Friday, nearly twelve years after the first revelation in Hira. The people of Madinah had long awaited his arrival and wanted to welcome him. The Prophet decided to stop where his camel halted. The camel stopped at a plot owned by two orphans—Sahl and Suhail. The Prophet

purchased the land from them and built a mosque there. The locals of Madinah, the Ansars, accommodated all Muslims, treating them as brothers. The Prophet assured the Jews of Madinah of their rights to life and

freedom of religion. He declared that Muslims and Jews would fight together if Madinah were ever attacked.

# Battle of Badr and Uhud

The Quraish planned a fresh attack on Madinah. The Prophet then gathered a small army to set out for Makkah. The battle took place at Badr. Though the Quraish had a larger army, the Prophet dreamt of them being far less in number. Since the Prophet and his warriors believed the enemy to be weak, they created havoc in the latter's camp, killing big leaders like Abu Jahl. The Muslims emerged victorious, though fourteen of them were martyred. The next battle between them took place on the plains and hills of Uhud. In this battle, some Muslim archers left their posts to attack the Makkans, against the instructions of Prophet Muhammad.

The Makkan cavalry took the Madinah army by surprise. The Battle of Uhud was a setback for the Muslims. Many Muslims, including the Prophet himself, were injured. Muslims had to wait for three years and rely on the Prophet's wisdom to win the next battle—the Battle of the Trench. Though outnumbered again, the Madinah fighters dug trenches

along the route of the enemy cavalry, greatly weakening it. In the end, after a tough battle, Muslims defeated their enemies and peace came to Madinah.

# Hajj and the Last Sermon

The Muslims had defeated the Makkans and both parties had agreed to peace. However, the Makkans failed to keep their word. In retaliation, the Madinah army laid siege to Makkah in AD 630. After the Makkans were defeated, the Prophet issued amnesty orders, pardoning the Makkans. This gesture won new converts to Islam, this time from Makkah.

The Prophet decided to perform Hajj. His pilgrimage to Kaabah completed, he delivered his last sermon at Mount Arafat where he told his companions that no Arab was superior to a non-Arab, neither was a white man superior to a black; all Muslims constituted one brotherhood. He reminded his followers that men and women had certain rights over each other and called women the "partners of men". He asked his followers not to take *riba* (interest), to follow the Quran and his own practices.

Upon his return to Madinah, the Prophet fell ill and passed away on June 8, AD 632 at the age of 63. He was buried at Masjid-e-Nabavi, one of the first mosques he had built in Madinah.

# OTHER TITLES IN THIS SERIES

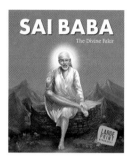

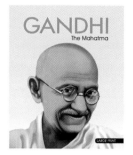

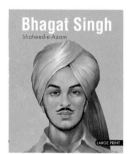

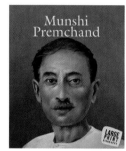

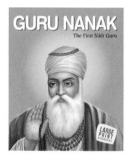

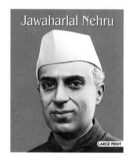

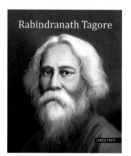

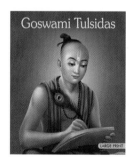

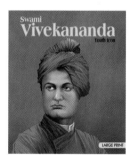

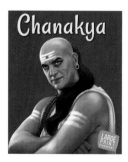